TRAVELS ON THE NOMADIC TERRAIN

PHILOSOPHY OF ACTION, DESIGN, AND
MULTIPLICITY
BOOK 6

DAN PAUL

PROACT 2525

CONTENTS

1

THE QUEST

At an early age, the contractions were too much to avoid. Proven over and over, the illogic of God, competition in schools, and authhority, it was too much. Somehow, the system was so bankrupt and still going. Everything disintegrates. Avoid this, that, and everything else; the pockets in the sand, the curly, golden locks of hair. The resistance set in, always looking for an expression it came out in these little bursts. Somehow, it had to become coherent. The flashes came and vanished. Moments that never seemed to end dissolved into a slow parade of time.

Bradley and the Bully Teacher

In grade school, a few memorable events were etched in memory. One was the day the teacher tied up Bradley. He ate lots of candy and couldn't sit still. He made noises and was fidgety. He got high from the candy. He was an offbeat kid. I never really bonded with him until that day. She stopped teaching and went to the back of the class. There he was, smiling, and she was resolute. She got the rope. It was one inch thick and about 20 feet long. She tied one end to the chair and wrapped Bradley in the rope; round and round it went. After that, he couldn't resist moving his lips, so she wrapped some tape around his mouth. There was Bradley in 2nd grade all tied up in Catholic elementary school. That memory set the stage for something else.

Robert and the Smack Hit

Another one from our school had a bit of prankster in his blood. He found clever ways to resist. A year before the 2nd-grade teacher subdued Bradley, Robert pulled a clever and unlikely stunt in the schoolyard. I wasn't expecting it because he didn't tell me he would do it. We were in the schoolyard, and recess was about to end in a few minutes. Robert gave me a signal to watch. I didn't have a clue what he was going to do. With his back toward me, he turned slightly and launched a soccer ball sky-high. My eyes followed the ball to the target. The first-grade nun got the ball squarely placed on her head. She buckled down for a bit and was OK shortly after. Somehow, the resistance got started.

Radar

A few years went by without significant action. Perhaps it was all in the minds of those who waited for the right time to act. They called him Radar. Maybe the name fits. Like many other names, Slimo, Hair Balls, Yeti, Scrangy, and Radar fit those muscles well. What provoked it, I don't know. I don't remember exactly being there, but my mind wasted little effort to imagine what it looked like or what had happened. Radar picked up one of the nuns and pinned her up against the blackboard. Forever, the image was etched into my mind. It was easy enough to go along with the crowd and obey enough to get through it. Everybody was going through the motions.

Pickin Rocks

The rocks were infinite. I was trying to figure out if I liked doing the work or if I didn't. Doing something was usually better than doing nothing, and why not? If you are getting paid, something is better than nothing. After elementary school and sometimes on Saturdays, they would pick us up, and we went to the farm. The barren corn fields had plants that were 4 inches tall. Killdeer would come every 20 minutes. We were given a five-gallon bucket to fill with rocks, carry to the flat trailer that a tractor was pulling, and empty the stones onto the trailer.

When the trailer was full, we drove to a low spot where we dumped the rocks. The harvesting machines would be destroyed in the fall if the stones were not removed. It was simple work. A kildeer bird could ease the boredom or the end of the field where we would have to turn around. We were paid 1 dollar per hour. If we were lucky, we would get some gloves. If not, our faces would be covered in dust, and our arms and hands would be loaded with fresh country farmland. We were picking rocks, building muscle, and the piggy bank.

Dr. Goodbar

What would Lucifer say, God or Marx, Malcolm X, Phillis Diller, the magic Pie man, and Faust, who meets Godot, then Quixote? I'm too selfish and too fuck you if you don't like how I look. I'm not here to please you or anyone else. If I have the chance to lend a hand, perhaps I will jump. Anyway, so yes, I've become aware of someone unknown as forever and yet more real than reality itself or AI, or BI anyway; so there's a person who is a being as real as you and I, flesh and blood, fingerprints, retinal scan, facial recognition compliant, certified Z monger looking for Dr. Goodbar.

Skating Without Ice

Somehow, it happened. Our school was at the roller skating rink. The wheels rolled across the flat space. It was dark in there. No windows anywhere. It was dark out, so no difference. The music played real high school music, the tension, the angst, the smell, the teenage guided conundrum. I could feel the heat. The urge came on. Without communication skills, something else had to speak. Somewhere, there was a target. When it broke, the satisfaction came. It didn't last, but it had to be there. It was a connection. Without language, what else could speak? The urge was strong but without ways of making it real.

Tripping in the Mine Field

We tripped on acid. The laughing would start and go on and on. Something was flipping and tripping. Keep it together. Reality was melting. Can I walk? Feel my face. Is it still there? It's melting. Wow, that's my color? Is this what other people are seeing? The vast mass of wires, like a Kafka novel. Crisp, lucid, like tangerine reality. The image kept coming back. It was a massive pyramid of bright fluorescent orange. A deep, swirling black maze surrounds the hill of Tang. On top of the mountain sat the grand master of desire without any splendor. Way up on top, a scene of the beach. The kaleidoscope magic umbrella and sunglasses are round, glazed with crystal mirrors, slim, and stacked, riding on the kangaroo walrus and tickled in pink, rosary spangled tie, twirling mist, rabbit, and dragon, loose wheeled, half dashed, and primed for another tomorrow. Did someone hit the reset button?

Vomit Lava

The party was planned. It was new. Married for 25 years, it was time to throw a party. People came dressed in their best. Threads fine, I walked the line. The steps would flow. The drinks were on the table, just sitting there. No big deal, so I tried one, then another, and another, and I kept flying around as if there were no consequences. Soon, it hit. My stomach started swirling. I was sitting at the table, anesthetized by the alcohol. Suddenly, it all came up. The stream of stench-laden lava began to roll across the table in a slow wave. My eyes wobbled in the sockets. What was next? Recovery mode? or keep on going? Quickly, the memory faded until I got out of the car. Was I still alive? My father said I was a man if I could reach the top of the stairs. Quick as greased lightning, I rose to the top, held up my arms to show my biceps, and declared, "I am a man." As my father laughed, I collapsed and suffered on the couch for three days from severe alcohol poisoning. The days wore on like quicksand. I was lying on the sofa, head swollen, swirling; when would it end?

Flashback to the Dark.

It was there in the window, just sitting there. The window was gone; it was there, next to me. I couldn't move. Paralyzed, I was shaking; my arms and legs could not move. The lion was huge, large enough to bite and crunch my neck with a quick whisk. It was right next to me. I couldn't do anything. A permanent stand-off. Like pushing a giant rock up the mountain. Fading, another reality came forth. Now, the gums and teeth were tingling. Yes, there was pain, like itching and frazzled disintegration. I could feel it, and it would linger. A prophet came and whispered. Trembling in the face of yesterday.

Reevaluation of all Values.

After high school and out of the yoke of the family, it was time for a reevaluation of all values. In Madison, it's possible to audit classes at the university. Few people were doing it. I looked up the classes I wanted and dedicated time and energy to get the most out of them. I took notes on the lectures and read the books, mostly on philosophy, politics, and history. Instead of writing papers, we started a zine called SMILE. In the magazines, we explored alternatives to the dominant codes. With an anarco-communist-situationist orientation, we called ourselves Schiz-Flux and did various art action events downtown and on the east side of Madison. With any extra time, I devoured books on philosophy by Kant, Hegel, Nietzsche, Deleuze and Guattari, and Situationists, Yippies, anarchists and others.

2

SOCIAL HOUSING

I landed after hitting too many dead ends. I got fired. I walked off the job. I didn't know what would happen. I walked. The last time, I was cutting a pipe after 14 12-hour days without a break. I was on an aluminum ladder. It was wet. I was welding and cutting, saw a spark, and woke up on the floor. The 220-volt shock blew me off the ladder. For a few moments, I was paralyzed. Electric shock is an uncommon pain. It's a bit of terror and a blast of the system of nerves. The wave of pain blew over. After that, it's moment to moment. It will be back. How long can I go without another smack? Usually, something happens 3-4 times per year. It's all about letting and getting the time to flow.

Transition

I got fired. It was the first time. Did I care? Fuck the boss. I had a duffle bag with checks. I was hoarding the checks. I had enough for 6 or 8 months of life. I could live off little, so why should I care? I knew my work was tops. It wasn't about that. It was a dead end. Money is a dead end. Jobs are slavery. I looked for an exit plan. I applied to the army. I could pick up another skill, make some money, and be ready for college. The army rejected me. So be it. If there was a draft, they couldn't get me. The last route was college. Knowing something more than nothing, I knew I had three choices for college: Berkeley, Austin, or Madison. Those were the most rebellious places I could think of. I never fit in anywhere, so the choice was obvious.

I landed in Madison on a beautiful fall day. The water gave light and life. I had no idea what to expect. With all those lakes, it had to be good. I put my fears on hold and continued. I got dropped off somewhere and started another chapter. I found housing and began applying for college.

U

The university was a foreign notion to me. I knew some general ideas but needed to process the internal logic of the actions. I didn't know the insider game that most had been groomed for since high school. I avoided all of that in high school. My background was in industrial construction work. I was picking rocks, welding steel, and framing houses. I found a job at a nuclear reactor lab. The biggest shock for me was the pace. It was like being on vacation compared to what I was used to. Suddenly, the world as I had seen it began to vanish. Basically, I was going from a neofascist work orientation to a social work orientation. I learned theories at the university and in the streets; in the coops, I learned practice. By the way, did you catch the rye?

L

The housing Coops in Madison liberate people from the housing exploitation of the dominant economy. I came upon them after my buddy moved out of our apartment. He told me about them, and I acted. I couldn't believe what I saw and experienced. It was a motley group of artists, idealists, intellectuals, and 1 or 2 people who had something like a regular job. We all worked together to make the project happen. We made housing for everyone. Owning, managing, and maintaining the building gave us enormous power. All we had to do was stick together. It was hard to believe how much we get for so little. Yes, it was a bit rough looking; yes, it was an egg that the hippies laid; yes, it liberated us from the constraints of capitalism, and yes, we were empowered more than any institution that had imprisoned our imagination.

How Can This Happen?

The core of the coop happens when members combine their minds to find solutions to own, manage, and maintain their housing. The decisions are socialized. Once a week, members combine brain power to determine their future. All are required to participate, but often it's just enough for a quorum. What's on the agenda? Whatever people put on the list. All are invited; imagine that happening at work, school, or family. All matters required to keep the coop running smoothly are on the agenda. Who will buy, prepare, and eat the food, do the dishes, clean the kitchen and living room, and sweep the sidewalk? Who will fix the door, do the treasury work, or take action to remove someone who has proven themselves unworthy of the coop? They must protect their lives from capitalism. If they don't maintain the building and pay for expenses, they will become fodder for the state capitalist housing methods.

Members Own Their Housing

I saw the revolution realized. If people own their housing, they don't have a landlord. The members determine how their building will be used. The buildings function for the members. The members decide how to use the building. Yes, they must follow the building and housing codes like everyone else. Unlike landlord housing, coops often have a workroom with tools and materials to maintain the building and bicycles. Coops frequently provide organic food, gardens, and wash lines for drying laundry and composting. Other amenities may include a meditation room, sauna, or lake access. The members decide. Immediately after joining a cooperative, you own the building. You own it without paying for it. It's free housing or as accessible as it gets. You pay to use and maintain it. You pay no profit. You keep the equity and use it to make other coops. If you don't want to own it anymore, you can leave. You won't get any money for the building. It's not market housing. Co-op housing has use value more than exchange value. It's for the members, not for capitalism. Social housing enables freedom from the economy. What is the wealth? It's housing that is secure and free from the economy.

The Landlord-Tenant Relationship is Loaded with Conflict.

Quietly as if nothing is happening, they operate 24/7, 365 days a year. Perfectly legal, following the rules, making long-term affordable housing. The Coops in Madison, WI, liberate people from the trappings of the landlord-tenant relationship. A product of capitalism, the idea that one person owns the apartment and another one lives there, is loaded with conflict. It produces evictions, homelessness, and wasted buildings and pushes the world to climate change extinction. Coop housing does the opposite. It teaches people how to own, manage, and fix their housing.

Members Own, Operate, and Maintain Their Buildings.

Coops are run by members who own, manage, and maintain the building. Becoming a member requires attending three dinners, passing a membership meeting process, filling out an application, paying the deposit, and signing the lease. Most Coop housing is 30-50% less than market-rate housing. Members meet once a week to make decisions about how to run the building. Typical topics are membership, work jobs, finances, events, and maintenance. Members must make monthly payments, do work jobs, come to meetings, and not bother anyone.

The Building

The Coops in Madison contain buildings with 7-20 rooms, a large kitchen, a living room, and 2-3 or more bathrooms. Members, not the landlord, decide what the rooms will look like, how they will be painted, what appliances and furniture they will use, and what changes to the building will happen. These decisions are made at the weekly meeting. Members are responsible for fixing any problems with the building. Often, members of the building can fix minor issues that arise. One work job is maintenance. Sometimes, 2-4 people do maintenance, with the most experienced person coordinating and directing the others.

The Culture

Coops cultivate a social and political culture that resists the dominant codes of conformity and authority that undermine a free expression of thought and action. With less pressure to earn money to pay for housing, members have more time to pursue life outside of a job. Coops confront bigotry. In the membership process, meetings, and conversations, people explore how to identify and transform bigotry into relationships that allow people to be whoever they are without reproducing white supremacy. Members engage in discussions that explore solutions to the vexing problems of capitalism. Beyond the pale, they can decide what to do with their common areas. Members decide whether or not they will use the building to have a party, support a social cause, or host workshops that advance sustainability in the community.

Becoming a Member

So, you want to become a communist? You've read the manifesto, are sick of working, and want to explore what is beyond the constraints of capitalism. This may work for you. Do you like manual labor? Are you a person who is easy to live with, work with, and make decisions with? Can you do essential jobs like fixing building problems, keeping the finances in order, or ensuring we comply with regulations? Coops usually require attending 2-3 dinners and meeting people to become members. If you get through that, the next step is to schedule a membership meeting. Any member can come to the meeting. At the meeting, they ask whether you can pay the monthly payments, do work jobs, and come to meetings. Other questions may explore how you deal with conflict, and your experience with Coops, and questions may show whether you have tendencies toward bigoted behavior. Some co-ops operate to reduce inequality in society. Be positive, practice responses, and take lots of deep breaths. It may go smoothly and efficiently, but typically, there will be a few tough questions. Be honest and focus on answering the questions the best way you can. They will tell you what the group has decided a day or two later. Typically, a majority of people at the meeting have to accept you. If you get rejected, don't take it personally. The group may be looking for someone completely different from you. If you make it in, keep your agreements. Pay on time, double the required work and attend meetings.

Work jobs

Work makes the Coop function and is the expression of the members. Some may scoff at doing work jobs. If that is you, a Coop won't work. The benefits of a Coop are a direct result of the work that people put into the coop. No work, no gain. Be positive about your work job. You have a lot to gain. Doing your work will advance your life and those around you. Living one year in a Coop will teach you more than ten years in college. Coop learning is immediately practical. The more you struggle, the more you gain. Work jobs include the following activities:

- -bookkeeping and finances
- -work job coordinator
- -clean up after dinner
- -cooking dinner
- -bread and granola maker
- -maintenance
- -board representative

Each coop determines the work jobs at weekly meetings. This will be set up when you arrive unless you start a new Coop. Usually, you keep the same work job for 3-6 months and switch after that. During that time, you learn to do the best work possible. The more you put in, the more you gain. If you need help with what to do, ask other members.

Coops are not for everyone.

Often, Coops contain single people and a few couples, and sometimes a couple with children. Can a big family work? Yes, if everyone agrees at a meeting. If you like to control every detail of the building, a Coop may not work for you. If you are a white supremacist, bully, or Republican, it's unlikely that a Coop is a good choice. Coops require communication and patience to make what the members decide. If you can't respect and follow other people's decisions in the coop, find another place to live. If you can only do work that immediately benefits you, live elsewhere. Coops require that you think and act in the interests of the coop. If you can't make the monthly payments on time, don't want to do your work jobs, or can't get along with people, save time and find another place to live. Coops require that you communicate well and respect the members.

Coops transform people

How can a Coop transform people?

- you learn to own, manage, and maintain your building
- you learn how to make decisions in a group
- you learn to live with other people
- you learn to consider the work and efforts of other people

People who live in a coop gain skills they've never had before and can use them for the rest of their lives. Decisions are made hierarchically in a family, at school, and work. At home, the parents call the shots; at school, you follow the teacher; and at work, the employer tells you what to do. In a Coop, each member has one vote. You put items on the agenda. In the group, you make decisions that affect your life and those around you. Making these decisions can make you prioritize what is most important for yourself and the group. Members determine how the building will be used. When members make decisions, they have to make solutions work. Whatever problems come up, you have to solve them with other members. When mistakes are made, they must be corrected. You feel the pain and have to make something work.

Coops Offer Housing Security.

With monthly payments of 30-50% less than market-rate housing, members can afford housing. For many people, that means they need to work less. While a few people like their low-wage jobs, many prefer doing other things. Some coops are members of a larger organization that coordinates cooperation between member coops and can take over if the members fail to keep the coops operating. If you are in a Coop that is part of several Coops, you may be able to get housing in those Coops if you need a change of pace. Madison Community Coop is one of those umbrella organizations. Phoenix, Marthas, and Hypatia are 3 of seven Coops in the organization. I remember stopping in and saying hello to people. Most of these Coops are easygoing about having other people over for dinner or using some of their amenities. As you get familiar with the place and people, it becomes easier to live there when a spot opens up. You aren't guaranteed a spot, but if people know you and the fit is good, it becomes another option that makes more security.

Skills That Last a Lifetime

People who have lived in a Coop learn to work with other people. Without reservation, they can see why they should work. They are familiar with Coops' decisions and won't need someone to explain why something must be done. They have skills that last a lifetime. They learn to ask for help and extend help to others without reservation. They gain housing security by solving the problems of owning, managing, and maintaining a building. Once you've lived in a co-op for a year, it will be easy to get into another co-op. Members learn to listen, communicate, and respect members at a meeting. Through meetings, you learn to think collectively. You learn to prioritize the issues and argue for what you believe is the best action for the coop. You set aside your interests to advance the group's interests.

Coops are Incubators of Idealism in Action.

Most Coops have a progressive orientation. Members are involved in various community-oriented social organizations that advance the means to meet needs sustainably in the community. Day and night conversations explore political and social issues at the forefront of society. Is it more important to buy local food or organic food? How can members address bigotry, sexism, racism, and homophobia in the coop and society? How can we set up housing education healthcare so that everyone has access?

Coops Liberate People from the Constraints of Capitalism.

For many people, working a job, paying for a car, and living in a landlord/tenant building is the recipe for an empty life of endless work, grinding away in a tedious, dead-end job. Coops reduce the cost of living while increasing the standard of living. With practical amenities like laundry, a workshop, a garden, and similar advantages, Coops offers a means to meet needs without endless work. Where can you live where people can live a more sustainable lifestyle? You often don't need a car when living in a Coop. Because people share a toaster, ten people don't need to buy a toaster. Most Coops purchase organic food for much less than if you lived in an apartment.

3

RAINBOW GATHERINGS

A band of hippies started the rainbow gathering in the 70's. The swelling rebellion against the Vietnam War, dead-end jobs, and the emptiness of consumer culture led to the great escape. The dominant culture was pushing for war, conformity, and boring lifelong marriage. Meanwhile, faced with the draft, seeing family and friends come home in body bags, and reading about the crimes committed during the war motivated waves of youth to embrace a way out. The pressure was intense and enormous. Somehow, they had to relieve the energy. Music, drugs, counterculture, and communes provided a way out. Throughout the country, especially on the west coast, the people of the Rainbow family met to generate another culture.

Connections

The rainbow gathering offers a connection to nature and the opportunity to live with like-minded people in a national forest for 1-3 weeks during the July 4th week. A starter group scopes out a location a month or 2 in advance. The gathering rotates locations. In a clockwise direction, it changes position every year. One year, it will be in the Midwest, next to the East, South, and West Coast. The challenges are many. Can the group nurture and prevent the dominant society from destroying it?

What?

How could such a gathering happen? Getting 5-20,000 people to visit a remote national forest is no small feat. Many people live next to nothing. They band together to make it work. Camping in a forest for a week or two requires significant planning. Some locations are cold at night and barely reach 70° during the day. Other places have lots of rain. The gathering is usually a mile or two from a parking lot or side of the road. People face natural dangers that are uncommon in the city. You must hike your food, water, and camping gear up and down hills and find a campsite. There's no grocery store for miles and no hospital or hardware store. If you make a mistake, it can create a lot of problems. Often, there's no Internet service or phone signal. So, for these rebels, that work was significant, and the challenges enormous. Nothing has been done like this before. No one had a permit.

Is it legal?

What are the rules in the national forest? There's no municipality, no plumbing, no electricity, no sewage, and no houses. Police are not close and are usually from a small town. The police were outnumbered and not trained to enforce whatever laws that may be applicable. At the gathering, there's a base camp where the vehicles are parked, and the main camp is accessible only by foot trails. The base camp is on the road and is accessible to the police. Most of the people are at the main camp. Either way, the Constitution still applies. People have the right to assemble. Without some legal basis, the group may easily have been intimidated to leave; however, like the Yippies, the hippies knew that they needed to have a group of lawyers available to beat back the police.

Motivation

If you might get drafted and sent on a suicide mission in Vietnam, perhaps you would be more likely to take chances. Indeed, the will to live became deeply embedded in these adventurous young people willing to do what had not been done. Inspiration came from the back to the land movement, where young people rejected the dominant society in favor of a fresh start in the countryside, where people could slow down and connect to the land, water, plants, and animals in a way that was impossible in the city. Other ideas explore applying theory to taking action and making the ideal real. Why not invite everyone to a national forest to camp out for a week and see what happens? It's a celebration of connecting to the land, living outside of capitalism, and experimenting to see if people can still make a life and culture beyond the dead-end society.

Preparation

People far and wide prepare for the gathering months in advance. Most join a camp where 10-50 people set up the means to live. Some plan to feed large groups of people. They arrange to buy, transport, and store the food without refrigeration and without letting the animals feast on the food. After getting the gear, food, and tools to base camp, they hike a mile or 2 to get to the main camp. All of this requires people power, which is uncommon in the city. People must behave the best they can. As your feet beat down the trail, it becomes apparent that you are on another mission into an unknown culture of your own making.

In the Beginning

A group of scouts starts a month or 2 in advance in a national forest to find a location with good sources of water, enough space to set up camps, and a mile or two from a road. Setting up a water source is the first goal. They find a wet area and trace it back to where they can set a pipe to tap the spring water. The pipe may be far from a camp. Ideally, there are water sources spread throughout the camp. Usually, you have to hike a block or two to get water. Is the water potable? Only sometimes, and getting sick at a rainbow gathering is easy. You may not be picky if your belly is empty and you're unsure where the next meal comes from. The scouts also look for areas to put the latrines. They must be a safe distance from the water. Pits are dug 3-4 feet down. Planks are placed across the holes, and people squat to defecate. Sometimes, they dig a trench about a foot wide, 3-4 feet deep, and 5 feet long. Mostly, there's little privacy, so you must let go of a squeamish orientation. Hygiene is less critical in dry climates than in wet locations like the Smoky Mountains. For people used to a toilet, the culture of the latrine requires some getting used to.

So Where's the Toilet? I Want My Toilet.

Yes, I want to feel the earth, so how can I do it without a toilet? If you're squeamish, you will have a chance to get over it. If you are part of the set-up crew in the beginning, you may be scoping out campsites and digging latrines. A latrine is a pit. Ideally, 3-4 feet deep and 2' x 3', or a trench 1 foot wide and 3-6 feet long and over three feet deep is suitable. People squat to let go of their digested food. The remains are covered with dirt, ashes, leaves, and compost. The pitt is covered with wood or suitable materials to prevent people from falling into the pit or trench.

Ethics in the Village

The idea is for people to help each other live well without money, shopping, and the conveniences of modern living. When someone needs help, you lend a hand. Participants must bring everything they need and take everything out when they go. At the end of the gathering, a group of people assemble to make sure all the trash is hauled out and make it look like no one has been there. It's a challenging job that may take a month or more. The culture after the gathering can be laid back.

Do's and Don'ts

Even though alcohol and drugs are frowned upon, alcohol is in the car camp. The Rainbow family has tried to influence people at the gathering to behave appropriately. Alcohol is banned in the main camp and is not seen very often. The car camp is another story. Some say it's a magnet for crime and drugs. Delinquent behavior is a police magnet and an excuse to shut down the gathering. People try to prevent it, but it's not easy.

Don'ts include, don't:

bring money

bring attitude

alcohol, drugs, and weapons

Do's, do this:

bring love, empathy, and compassion

bring food for two or more

bring medical supplies

be bright, cheerful, and full of energy

bring camping gear

Sweat Lodge

Usually, there's a sweat lodge where people can cleanse their bodies of toxins while experiencing a ritual of native cultures. The hut can take different shapes depending on the location and availability of materials. Some lodges are 20' in diameter, circular, with a 3-foot high wall. Mud straw and clay are used for the walls and a mix of branches and tarps for the roof. A hole in the wall is cut for people to enter. In the middle of the hut is a pit where they bring superheated rocks. A fire, which is outside of the sweat lodge, heats stones, and at the right time, they are carried into the hut.

Safety in the Sweat Lodge

It's crucial that you are prepared for a sweat lodge. It can be a very draining experience. It would help if you properly hydrated yourself. This means getting enough water, which has to be free of pathogens. Try to bring 2 quarts of water. Also, you need to have electrolytes. This is very important because you sweat a lot. Electrolytes include salts and sugars. Crackers and fruit juice can do the trick. It gets sweltering in the sauna. Some people push it and make it very hot, and they may not want you to leave during the ritual. It's a whole experience.

Herbs may be placed on the rocks, and then water quickly fills the lodge with steam. One idea is to push your body to withstand intense heat. The combination of heat and healing compounds from the herbs can produce a lot of sweat, which clears the body of toxins and destroys pathogens that cause illness. Some sweat lodges are near a cold water source like a lake, river, or ocean. After superheating in the lodge, you can go into the freezing water and get a shock that can boost your circulation, enhance your skin, and give a big jolt. The mud, herbs, and rocks generate an experience outside a typical sauna. Sometimes, the host makes prayers. A sweat lodge can test your limits. If you have any health issues, ask if you can enter last so you can quickly get out. It's easy to get dehydrated, so you must take caution when using the sweat lodge.

Spirit of the Camp

A range of people come to the camp. Some are running from the law, but most often, they are in the car camp. Many have been bruised, battered, and abused by parents, teachers, bosses, the Church, and other institutions of the dominant society. Others, more fortunate and able to make a positive space, come with an orientation to practice what an ideal community would look like. How can we live a non-fascist life where people give what they can and take what they need? How can we live without injuring or destroying the air, land, water, plants, animals, and people?

Children's Camp

Filipe often ran the children's camp. It was another refuge from what could be a little too much: adults. Children are the focus, with lots of love, attention, and praise. A core group directs volunteers to watch children, make food, do dishes, and make people happy. When possible, Filipe would drive the bus to a camp location. The bus was packed with food and supplies to make the camp run. It was colorful, with a spirit of love and care.

Camps

Camps are groups of 10-50 people who make a camp, often to make food or provide a service like the Calm Mash tent. Usually, camps are from a geographic area. There's the fairy camp, Hari-Krishna camp, Kickapoo camp, and others.

First Aid

The rainbow gathering moves toward a self-sufficient village, which means they strive to take care of all their problems in the community. To take care of people who are injured or sick and to track the health of the camp, a calm/mash camp is set up. Organizers gather what they can to set up supplies and equipment to address the health problems.

Most issues they deal with are minor, but if they can't handle it, they will find a way to get those in need to the hospital. Stomach-related problems have a solution at the camp. Dealing with aches and pains, sprains and bruises, and whatever comes their way is the play of the Calm/Mash camp.

The Feather of the Governess

The rainbow family uses elements of other cultures. People gather in a circle in the center of the camp. The person in the middle raises the feather when they speak, and everyone listens. When the speaker is finished, people raise their hands, and the speaker gives the feather to the next person. The feather may symbolize governing with a feather, light, strong and sensitive. Listening is a way to show respect for the feather. It's the voice of those who care to speak and contribute to what makes the village weather the storm to stick together and create a holistic and sustainable community. It's governing with the lightness of a feather. The opposite is a fist. Feather governing is about listening as if you can hear the lightness of a feather, which is the voice of everyone who has spoken. As you take something, as you make something, as you ponder how you take action, you take action with the ideas of the feather, all those words that have been spoken.

Making Decisions

Rainbow people must make decisions. The idea is to make decisions by consensus. Everyone must be given a chance to speak and be heard. One version of consensus is that consensus has been reached when the feather has been passed, and no one else wants to talk.

Media

I found out about the rainbow gathering from another person. They told me about it face-to-face. They didn't use a flyer. There's no address. Often, the location is something you search for by word of mouth. It's hard to imagine that something like this would work at this time in place. Many rainbow families keep a low profile. As the Rainbow family gained more experience, they were able to make traditions. This can reduce the amount of decisions that have to be made. One decision is where the next gathering will be held. The location follows a circular pattern, going clockwise around the country. It started in the West, then moved to the Midwest, the following year to the East, and then to the South. If the same people participate in the decision-making, they know where the most likely locations are and don't have to figure it out again.

Food I'm Hungry

Remember, there are no restaurants or grocery stores at the rainbow gathering. Typically, most people join a camp and help make food for all the people in the camp and some extra for those in need. This is no small task. The kitchen areas are typically under a gazebo that the camp sets up. Often, this is a structure of wood posts that people lash together with a roof that is made with a tarp. Better kitchens are organized to maintain good hygiene in a camp that rarely has hot water or an endless supply of cold water. Often, people cook large pots of food that require a lot of ingredients, which must be hiked in from the car camp. With enough discipline and production, the Krishna camp can make a lot of food to serve in the late afternoon. It's Indian, often vegan, sometimes tasty and sweet, and loaded with carbs. It was typically an option where you didn't have to feel like a sponge when showing up to eat.

Car Camp

The car camp is located near the road in an area large enough to park vehicles people use to get to the gathering. Some people want to avoid hiking a mile or 2, so they hang out at the car camp. With a vehicle, it's easy to get alcohol. Carrying alcohol to the main camp is often too much for people who drink beyond considerations of health. Where there's alcohol and poverty and rednecks, someone will likely get too excited. When this happens, someone may call the police. A threshold has been crossed, which may bring more heat. Some had a code to alert people about the police coming. They would say "6up," and everyone would repeat it, and quickly, people would know that the police were in camp. This would intimidate the police and prevent them from being ambushed by the police.

Hassle From the Authorities

How can so many people meet and not need a permit or permission from authorities or the government? The wise ones who started the project relied on the Constitution. All gatherings are held in national forests. The law of the land says that people shall have the right to assemble. Now, if the Rainbow family leaves a big mess in the forest or if they didn't take care of each other and had to rely on local authorities, or if they bothered a lot of people, perhaps those who can't stand naked hippies in the woods may use that as a pretext to hassle and arrest people. Thousands of people show up for these events. They are located in remote areas, so it would take a small army to put all those people in prison. And who is bothered by 5-15,000 Rainbow people camping in a forest that few people know exists? The Rainbow people have lawyers on their side and have won more than a few cases. The gathering has been happening for many years, so it has a significant track record of conducting a safe, peaceful event without leaving a mess. So, primarily, the authorities leave it alone.

Radical Action

The gathering is a radical event in which people live without money and depend on each other's support to survive. People set up camps based on location, like the Kickapoo camp in southwest Wisconsin. Other camps are based on affiliation, like the Hare Krishna camp. Some are 5-10 people, and others are much larger.

Bigotry

The problems of the dominant society don't magically disappear when people enter the forest. Bigotry knows no boundaries. Sexist men are a common problem. The gathering is often 90% white, so non-white people may feel like outsiders, and some may not feel welcome. Please treat everyone as brothers and sisters; show love, kindness and respect to make a rainbow family.

Some celebrate the Fourth of July, which is more than a bit ironic since a lot of the orientation of the camp is to set up something beyond the dominant culture. The myth of the rainbow gathering is that every fourth of July, somehow, there is a rainbow. If you have a lofty idea of what a camp is, including anywhere with a rainbow on the 4th of July, the reality of the illusion could become real. It's a celebration of the coming together of difference and authenticity as people cultivate unity with nature.

Barter Village

Barter is allowed in the village. It's not the most significant event and borderline creeping capitalism, but it may have some roots in native cultures. Hot items at the circle vary. Whatever it is, people hope to have the most desired objects. The options are limited because everything must be hiked in a mile or two from the car camp. The best people can do is make something valuable and beautiful from what they can find on the land. You may know how to find mushrooms or whittle a souvenir from a special tree or plant. Candy bars can be as popular as bracelets and jewelry. The barter circle typically has between 10 and 25 people selling what they don't want to take out and what will most likely get them what they want. It's usually on a path that provides a bit of difference in a camp without money.

Living without clothing is acceptable for those who like it and others who don't. After all, who needs all those clothes when it's hot, and what if you want a tan in your private areas? Is unwanted attention a concern? Yes, it's probably a good idea to do it with friends or when others are doing it, and mostly, if it's welcomed.

Critical Perspective

The opportunism of the dominant culture has undermined the idealism of the past. The power of the flower may be hampered by those looking to take advantage of the lack of police and security. Many are collateral damage of capitalism. These are white people who have the privilege to take off work and act like hippies for a week. When they get home, they destroy the world the same way the rest of the world does.

Peace and Love

Can the rainbow gathering make peace and love amid all the chaos of capitalism? Many beat-down people are attracted to the gathering. They have a lot of problems. With drugs and other methods, they tried to relieve the pain. Others have more to give. They come with peace, love, and a vision of another world. A world in which people care for each other as much as they care for themselves, a world in which people become the change they want to see, a world in which plants, animals, and people live harmoniously with the air, land, and water. With naïveté, innocence, and a sublime presence, they walk a path of many dangers on the way to peace, love, and happiness.

Rainbow Liberation

Rainbow gatherings offer a chance to experiment with another reality. Have you ever wondered, "What would happen if we all lived together in the woods for a week without the pressure of production and consumption? Can people make another reality of living light on the land, cultivating relations with the air, land, water, plants, animals, and people more than screens, plastic, and fake reality?" The Rainbow Gathering is a rebellion against the dominant codes of conformity, consumption, and dead-end work that pushes humanity into global warming extinction. For many, the gathering is the ultimate way to transform relationships that destroy the environment and living entities. Here, the focus is on gratitude over attitude, peace over conflict, and adaptation over mindless consumption.

4

VEGAN ACTION: MEETING NEEDS FOR FREE

Strategically, they bought the building. A mix of drag queens and idealists combined their energies to make a place where people actively decided and acted on this question, "What is the best life that can be lived?" Meeting needs locally and sustainably was one answer. Another is to make a space where the ultimate freedom is realized: freedom from the economy. Here, people are not required to live according to the capitalist machine. Over the years, another way of life emerged. They made every day an operation to help meet needs sustainably, locally, and in the community. We made a homeless shelter, gave food to people in need, and published information to help people find housing, healthcare, and food.

1989 Anarchist Gathering in San Francisco

In 1989, a group of anarchists, rebels, and punks invited non-fascist-minded people to share their lives and actions. Workshops focused on living outside the dominant reality in ways that avoid, confront, and make alternatives to the capitalist machine. The gathering was loaded with differences. Cells, a group of 4-5 people, explored alternative sex, gender, and economic ways of living. Queers, punks, hippies, and rene-gades collaborated to make smooth-running information-sharing sessions where people learned how to set up housing, food, and medicine for people in need. Here, cooperation and mutual aid combine to advance action worth doing. I came across the group when I went to a workshop on economics. We learned why it's essential to undermine the exchange economy with the free economy. No events or activities were held in the commune unless the guiding principle "no one turned away for lack of funds" was adhered to. Everything, which includes meeting needs, was done for free.

Radical Action

The members created the most radical project in the US. Within a non-straight culture, vegan food and a focus on meeting needs for free, the commune practices being the change you want to see. No detail is left to chance. Quality is queen. Members dedicate themselves to the project. Periodically, as needed, a meeting was held. At the meeting, people suggested and planned ways to improve the projects they worked on.

Vegan Orientation

In the commune, all food is vegan. People cook and serve food to all who are present. Augmented by the trees, bushes, and gardens, the produce is the central star of the table. Like other communes, the food and etiquette are not fetishized. People are free to eat at their pleasure. Non-vegan food does not enter the building. Have you ever had tofu that tastes like barbequed spare ribs? Without gender constraints, men were allowed to cook, clean, and embellish the pleasures of the flesh.

The Roots of Radical Action

Inspired by the Shakers, Diggers, and Mother Teresa, the group evolved into a grassroots organization to advance the means for people to live outside the capitalist machine. The group set up a homeless shelter, published the free eats and shelter charts, and made a free vegan meal each week for people who were hungry. The path the commune took was a shortcut to the Marxist ideal where people give what they can and take what they need, and eventually, the state withers away as people meet their needs sustainably in the community.

The Split

The '60s were a period of upheaval. Traditions, bashed and broken, gave way to other ways of living. Should the group be used to get dressed up, take acid, do theatre and have an orgy? Or should members enrich the spirit by dedicated service to those in need? The tensions between these currents of action were ongoing. The libidos of those in motion weren't limitless. What do you do after the party is over? Parties become hackneyed repetition if there's nothing between. There's no difference. Also, if one group is partying, you end up with one group that parties and one that performs. People can do both, but after the party is over, the hangover begins. The hard-core pleasure gang gave way to those dedicated to meeting needs.

Soup Kitchen

In the early 1990s, the commune had a weekly soup kitchen. On the large kitchen table were mountains of vegetables that we chopped, diced, and sliced to make soup, salad, and vegan meals. It was well organized and operated efficiently. Servers wore makeshift tuxedos, and women wore the gorgeous and the fantastic. Before, in-between and later bits of cabaret gave an exotic twist to the core of culture in the heart of the Mission district. As time passed and gentrification spread, some prominent people faded away. When people started coming to the event in limousines, it became apparent that the fundamentals of serving the poor drifted into serving those with too much. As this happened and they remodeled the lower area into a homeless shelter, they began making soup, bread, and salad and serving it to people in need in downtown San Francisco.

Publishing and Bookbinding

The commune is not a bimbo capital. The largest room was a library that doubled as a sleeping area. Why not sleep among books? Imagine Emma Goldman waiting for Godot. The commune published street sheets in the 60s and later a book of writings and drawings of the members. They printed the book using an offset printer, which requires advanced skills. This was very technical, meticulous work. They were absolute sticklers for detail. Never spoken, somehow, the idea of perfection was there. Quality was achieved with attention to every detail. Eventually, the focus of publishing became the free eats and shelter charts, which were distributed to 400 social service organizations in San Francisco.

Meetings

Meetings at the commune explored topics and concerns to make the ideal real. Action doesn't happen from nothing. The commune was made with thinking, collective thinking. Ideas go nowhere if they are not defined to the point of action. Meetings took the idea and made it real. Where and at what time should soup be served to homeless people? How do I get the truck, computer, and car fixed? What should we do with members who are out of bounds? Go far and wide, and you'll never find a project like this. Only a few communes are vegan, and few are dedicated to helping needy people. Meetings are a critical part of the commune.

Under the Radar

By the time I arrived, the commune had undergone many permutations. Members came and left. The heydays of the beginning had given way to a persistent and dedicated practice of meeting needs sustainably in the community. The doors were open in the beginning, and many came and left. The street sheets they made and distributed in the '60s led to more activity. Eventually, the wide-open approach caused too many problems. In the peace and tranquility of the commune, there was less need for more people. Again, it's about quality. Some people are ready; others have yet to arrive or probably never will be. Eventually, the commune kept a low profile. Making the means to live for free can generate too much attention, undermining the project's goals. Keeping a low profile helps keep the project functioning.

Permaculture in the Mission

Imagine walking out of your kitchen onto a second-story deck, reaching up, and harvesting avocados. The ideals of the commune were realized in various ways. The area has grown into a permaculture paradise with carob and almond trees on the street and apple, plum, apricot, and avocado trees in the backyard. Annuals, perennials, trees, and bushes are home in the backyard. The soil of the paved area of the lumberyard has been liberated and gets water, light, plants, and animals. The commune increased green space in the city.

Going to the Food Bank

The process of living at the commune was a continuous series of rituals. After doing something a hundred times, habits evolve into a constant flow, where there's less adventure and more nuance of details that take on meaning only after doing the same thing day after day, week after week. I didn't make the tradition as much as carry it on. The pioneer's phase had passed many years ago. Now, it was about fine-tuning the big machine. Such was the food bank. The tree had a list that was mostly in mind; I had muscles and brains ready for action. We loaded ourselves in the truck and headed for the food bank. It's a large, warehouse-type building with stocks of food donated by those with too much for those with too little. The food bank was stocked with tofu, olives, bread, and a range of produce. Tree chose the items, and we loaded the truck and went back to the building. The goal was to buy enough food to make a bag or two of vegan food to give away.

The Food Giveaway

I didn't realize what can happen when you give away bags of food. If you served some item the group wanted, like Asian pears, vegetarian fillet mignon, or super chocolate cookies, there was a chance the line could turn into a mob, which would not be so pretty and undermine the purpose. Also, do you put all the items into a bag and give each person a bag, or should volunteers serve items? If you serve the items, you may have many leftovers, so you have to fill the truck, restock the items, and somehow find a way to use the food before it goes bad. If you give away bags of food and people have items they don't want, they could leave them on the sidewalk. Also, you have to set up tables and clean up later. If you leave a mess, the neighbors will complain. If someone getting food is rude to people in the neighborhood, it is more likely that you could get shut down. In San Francisco, most urban spaces are occupied and well-used, so finding a spot where enough people will show up and not bother anyone is another challenge.

Free Eats and Shelter Charts

Eventually, the focus of publishing was to help people in need with information. If I'm hungry in San Francisco, where can I get food? If I'm homeless, where do I get shelter, or if I need healthcare or my teeth fixed, how can I do that? The free eats, shelter, medical, and fix-it charts have been published for over 20 years. Each page or two lists where, when, and how to get what you need. The charts tell you when and where to get free cooked meals, free pantry items, and free medical and mental health help. The charts are a way for people to get the help they need. Online sources of information have now replaced the charts.

Beyond Working into the Fabulous

While reading and exploring the intellect were pursued, members were no strangers to the pleasures of the flesh. During the '60s, before the group was formed, they would dress in drag and perform. Some people took LSD to enhance the experience. The commune had an extensive selection of drag costumes and makeup. They made props, got dressed up, and went to the park. Most of the performances were loose compositions at the edge of the theatre.

Technical and scholarly

The commune had a generous level of technical expertise. Quality is never compromised. Every detail is magnified, contemplated, and carefully attended to. Every number is essential. If someone is an hour late because of a typo, and it's their only chance to get a meal for the day, is that important? The commune practiced helping people get food, medicine, and housing in all work, from construction to publishing, from preparing and serving food to greeting people at the door.

The commune was a shining star of radical action to meet needs sustainably in the community. With decades of experience and projects that helped thousands of people, the commune took action to meet their needs. Through years of defining what is essential and how to do quality work, they refined methods to get thoughtful work done.

5

BOLOZONE

In 1996, I offered a charette of action called "Compositions in Multimediaction" as part of the School for Designing a Society (SDAS). The idea was to compose a project to generate radical art and action. One person, Dan, showed up. He was pleasant, open, and free of agendas. Both of us were a part of SDAS, so we needed no introductions to use composition to make actions. Think of the question, What is experimental today? What are the conditions for radical art and action to happen? So, that day, I talked with Dan about those two questions.

St. Louis

Over the last year, another participant in SDAS, Mark, had spoken about St Louis. The city sold houses that needed work for a low price. St Louis offered opportunities but also intense crime and poverty. The town was ripe for some new energy. We kept hearing about the artists in the area and the history of the struggle to get the city to function at a higher level. Activists were calling on the city to respond faster to emergencies and fires. At the time, they had to wait 30-40 minutes to get a response. By that time, someone could be dead, or the building burnt beyond repair. With ears open on the action, Dan and I came to focus.

Bolo Bolo and Zone

Bolo Bolo is a book by PM. The book explores making a bolo, an autonomous area in a city where people live outside the constraints of the consumer-oriented world of production and consumption. The project moves toward creating a self-sufficient urban space of 400 people. The goal is to establish autonomous regions beyond the pale of domestication and work for the money machine. Zone is an independent nonprofit publisher of books that span philosophy, history, and political and social theory. The books integrate art design into a philosophy book. Zone books cross the boundaries between philosophy, art, and design.

Bolozone

The Bolozone is a combination of the ideas of the book Bolo Bolo and the Zone publisher's books. The idea is a play of difference and interaction between an autonomous zone in Bolo Bolo and a field of action from the Zone books. So, how would that manifest itself? What would this be in flesh and blood, and sticks and stones? How can you make a Bolozone? Eventually, we found a house in a neighborhood close to artists we knew. I funded the project with my savings, and Dan offered to live there. I would help from a distance and go there when he needed me to do construction work. We had been involved in alternative projects where a strong leader would take over and dominate the project. That was something both of us wanted to avoid. It would not be my fiefdom or his, which is another reason to name the project. It's not Dan's house, and it's not Jane's house; it's the Bolozone. What's the Bolozone? The Bolozone is community-oriented housing for radical artists and activists.

Nomadic International

In the mid to late 1980s, a group of people became attracted to living in Bolozones around the world. The idea is to set up a base on every continent. Each base or Bolozone would have housing for core members and travelers. It would also have a progressive, radical, or sustainable project that people could participate in. Funding would come from donations, fundraising, and money for housing. People who live there would pay for expenses, including taxes, insurance, utilities, and maintenance. Visitors would also pay per night. The project would adhere to the principle, "No one turned away for lack of funds." We circulated the idea to friends and found someone willing to let us use her lot in Quito, Ecuador, for the first international Bolozone. While the idea was quite appealing, there were many challenges—funding and who wanted to live outside the US and set up such a project. While I liked the idea and would be willing to work on it from the US, I wasn't ready to give up my life and go there. Dan was more open to going there but had more than enough commitments.

Composition in Multimediation

So, I met with Dan at a workshop I did titled Experiments in Multime-diaction. We talked about how we didn't want to be armchair people. Somehow, this had to take a physical shape. So, by combining the opportunity of St. Louis and the ideas of Bolo Bolo and the Zone books, we came up with the Bolozone. The Bolozone would be a place for radical artists and activists to live and make art and action. Like the most radical coop in Madison called Nottingham Coop, we would present ourselves as the place for radical artists and activists to live and do their work. We would buy a building from the city, fix it, and offer it to artists and activists to live.

3309

Dan and I found a building at 3309 Illinois. With a little effort, the city sold it to us. It didn't need much work, but enough to be more than a challenge. One by one, we worked through the problems. At one point, the toilet no longer functioned. With no other options, we called a plumber. The plumber reamed open the line. Within 5 minutes, the contents of 2 months of using the toilet came up over the toilet and filled the bathroom with 4 inches of raw sewage. The smell was nause-ating. With no other options, Dan and I scooped the poop and hauled it into the dumpster in the back. In a couple of hours, we had it cleaned up. The sewage couldn't go anywhere because the line from the city to our building was broken. We called the city and got it fixed, and now all the flushes are royal.

A Mighty Hot Day and a Fire

Another day, we were working at the back of the building, and I took a nap. When I woke, I could smell smoke. Dan yelled, "Fire in the back!". I jumped fast as lightning. I wanted to put out the fire before the fire department got there. I opened the back door and saw flames going up the back side of the building. With adrenaline in high gear, I yelled at Dan to set up the hose and spray from above. As he set that up, I battled the fire from below. I worked on the fire with what I could find: a fire extinguisher, water, and a rug. We had just finished working on the back, and now it was on fire. There was no way I was going to let it spread. A power line was right above the fire. If the fire hit the roof, it would be all over. With the hose, Dan took the heat from the fire with water from above. In a few minutes, it was over. The fire lost, and we won. If I had waited 5 minutes, we would have lost the building. The wood framing was very old, and the asphalt roofing burns quickly. Later, we realized someone had put a bunch of couches back there, and the next day, they started on fire.

Police for Monsanto Attack the Bolozone

Over the years, various anarchists and activists have lived in 3309 Illinois. At one point, Monsanto was making another attack on the environment. Activists from around the area gathered at the Bolozone. In 2003, they used the Bolozone as a base to provide housing and support for the activists opposing Monsanto. Eventually, the police came, arrested people, and vandalized the Bolozone. A flurry of press exposed the police misconduct as public support for the activists increased. The Bolozone project supports radical artists, activists, and cultural workers to realize their projects while integrating and helping the community.

The Function of the Bolozone

Cultural workers, artists, activists, writers, musicians, and others are rarely paid. A few make it to the top, while others work to advance the culture of the community. They can't afford market-rate housing. The Bolozone is set up for artists to get affordable housing. Artists and activists learn to own, manage, and maintain their buildings. They build up equity to make their lives more secure. Equity in the house can be used as collateral to get loans and buy another building. With less money spent on housing, artists have more time to make art. They don't have to work two jobs to pay for expenses. That's the purpose of the Bolozone. The idea is to set up the conditions for radical art and activism to flourish. There are more than a few urban areas with high crime, poverty, and low-cost housing. If artists, writers, and activists learn to own, manage, and operate their housing, they should have more time to do their art.

6

SCHOOL FOR DESIGNING A SOCIETY (SDAS)

I was living at Dreamtime Village, and a group of engaging composers showed up. It was like the stork brought them. I couldn't imagine a more fascinating group of people to become aware of. When one of the organizers saw that I was washing dishes, I immediately became a default celebrity, which is, by any measure, an astonishing achievement. This labor was common. I was doing it all the time. Anyway, the school visited us and taught us about the most happening culture in the US.

SDAS began in 1991 and was started by Marianne Brun, Mark Enslin, Susan Parenti, and others who sought to make another world possible. Rooted in composition and theatre, the group stayed with us for a week. An uber inspiration in the middle of nowhere WI, a group like this comes to visit once every decade if I'm lucky. I finished the load of infinite dishes and wondered who would appear next. I'd never been famous for washing dishes.

Imagine

Imagine a society that you would want to live in. Could it be a scene out of a science fiction movie, the Garden of Eden, with two chairs, a table with some wine and cheese, and two people discussing what would happen if Waiting for Godot met My Dinner with Andre?

Many people can say what they don't want, but can you say what you want? What if someone offered you a chance to design an urban area of your choice? They gave you 3D printers, robots, chickens and goats, you name it, anything. Would it be purple, yellow, or fluorescent orange with cream lipstick? What if in that secret stash of desires was a list of questions you wished someone would ask you? In your dream, you were stuck in a wonderland to make the life you've always wanted, something more than a favorite food with a chocolate sauce and a dash of bitters, or a tender glance from a person of interest, or the flower of a thousand nirvana that triggers eternal, full body orgasms? Could life be another world? Did Faust leave for an appointment with Don Quixote and Marilyn Monroe? The riddle lets Genie out of Pandora's box, and then?

Springing into Time

Suddenly, our little village came alive. I couldn't figure out who to be more inspired about. Could we meet them all? Would they give me one second? Some were so ethereal, focused on their little world; how could I get their attention? Me an anti-appearances outlander from Nowheresville, USA. I could do a seminar on washing dishes. Typically, each one could play at least one instrument very well. Each one was like a deity, really, in our village. It was beyond a dream come true. I still can't believe it happened. Eventually, fantasy became a reality. They had a whole lineup of activities planned. We met on the 2nd floor of the school. It was beyond perfect, with large windows overlooking the garden and a small library. They danced without prancing, sang without singing, and performed compositions, stunning us with intellectual excursions into social action and designing a society.

"Things are what is said about them," Herbert Brun.

Language describes events and history. The language people use can define the choices people make. It's easy to repeat how events are framed in the dominant media, but what if it's about you, and they get the story backward? If you don't tell your story, someone will tell it for you to advance their project. The crucial task of describing what happens for and by ourselves can make the difference between our work being seen as worthless and mediocre or a significant and valuable contribution. Documenting our work in words and images is a historical record of what happens. If you want your work to go somewhere, composing what it's about is essential. Don't let other people frame your work before you. The initial imprint may be challenging to erase.

Composition

As a core idea in the school, composition is an offer to explore chaos to create something that would not exist without us. To compose is to generate a difference, antagonize, provoke, and harass what we assume in order to develop alternatives. The act of not knowing is an area ripe for exploration and experimentation, a path to wander around in, to feel the chaos, define a domain, inhabit the domain, and become something else to generate difference. Composition explores a system to extract information. The "retardation of decay "(Herbert Brun) is a process of interaction within a domain that extracts information in ways that maximize the positive potential. Composition is engaging a phenomenon or a realm of chaos to create a domain in which the resource is exhausted. Composition creates that which would not exist without us.

Learning Methods

Learning can be a direct linear experience that involves engaging multiple directions. People learn differently. Engaging desire is a form of learning that embraces motivation instead of content while avoiding obedience and following codes that lead to the dominant institutions. The path is not prescribed and may lead to unexpected areas or repeat what has been or what is. SDaS is a learning experiment that embraces desire as fuel. One method focuses on creating 'assignments' for friends. Here, an assignment is a gift. Sometimes, friends can imagine areas for another move, which could be the ticket to significant differences. Assignments can be received more as an offer than a demand. Of course, this requires an enlightened friendship free of the dark side of competitive relationships, fashion famines, or relentless repetition. Can you color in C minor? To give an assignment is to provide a gift, a thoughtful encounter with an ironic dilemma, or a problem without solutions. SDaS is an obstacle course of blockages for desire to negotiate, undermine, disrupt and channel into difference. A shared community of people investigating the desired action connection creates a flow. If you can ride the flow, learning becomes the process of engaging now.

80th birthday

The school spread its seeds far and wide. On Herbert Brun's 80th birthday, a week-long set of events brought alums back to Urbana to play compositions. For me, it became a significant event in composing and avant-garde music history. I had yet to learn who would play what or how. I was baffled by the sounds. These are ones that I've never experienced using instruments I've never seen before. This was like each musician made another universe to inhabit, extracted the best of what they could find, and laid it out like a five-star dinner. Day after day, it happened, and I kept wishing that they could spread it out over half a year. After all, how many 5-star meals can you eat in one day?

Seminar in Experimental Composition

What is experimental today? What have you done that would not exist without you? If you want something, how do you create the conditions so that it will exist? The seminar was the core class at the school. Most of the time, I was stumped. I came up with a few things. Stumping is a process in which your mind goes into a field of chaos, this clumsy, oblique haze. Eventually, you mine information, which becomes the core of the composition.

Anti-Porn Class

I went to the anti-porn class. Men were not allowed to speak. The instructor repeated the same thing over and over. It wasn't impressive. It felt like he was ramming down my throat. More inspiring was a man I found online who embraced masculinity. He was wacky and full of energy. He wasn't against being a man. So what does that mean? Embrace your manliness until you have no room for porn. He was upbeat and encouraged men to do the things that make us more manly. As this happened, you would forget about porn. What does that mean? Let's say you realize the pleasure you get when playing sports, then play more. Maybe you are good at sewing, then become more passionate about that. The idea is to cultivate and celebrate the person you are. Engage in desiring action, and develop a desire to realize something you want more than anything else. It is positive. Making habits that make challenging things the most invigorating with the most pay off in the long run. He said you can fill your life with activities with a bigger payoff, which may not be this year or next, but that's when the investments may generate the highest returns. He was wacky, funny, colorful, and charismatic.

Urban Permaculture

Robert grew urban permaculture in Urbana. Here is yet another shining star in the village. With pleasure and finesse, Robert could easily do what the best struggle with. How can this unmacho guy defy the laws of ill-logic and anti-cacaphony? So in a short while, Robert produced bushels of produce, including daikon radish, kale, collards, and that weird tomato tree, or Rumplestilskins rabbit foot carrots from Siberia. So, what does permaculture have to do with it? Just like the song, it grew melodies out of the plants. The opera of nothing + the science of imaginary solutions + a one-way ticket to nirvana =, of course, you guessed it, drum roll, please. Robert asked people with unused backyards or land if he could grow food for anyone who desired. A standard answer was yes, and more than a few of us came together looking fresh, alive, and energized from?? Robert's urban permaculture magic show!!!

Art Class

On Saturday morning, we went to art class. Again, Robert was there, and the host, a beautiful, soft-spoken, well-talented man from Ethiopia, Gossa, set the conditions for us to explore what we could do with paint and a brush. Often, it was outside. It was a modest location enveloped in a subtle choice of colors, textures, and placements, and it was uniquely non-American. This is a welcome respite from the hackneyed culture of consumption of plastic fantasy land where all happiness can be achieved through consumption. Supplies were provided for people to paint, usually outdoors and in the basement in the winter. The friendly, cozy, mostly noncompetitive area was a nest for relaxed collective creativity. There was more Fela than conversation and more art than arguments. It was here that I was inspired to paint. I produced a series of ten paintings, which I eventually put into frames displayed at the On the Job Center. OJC is a collective of like-minded artists who do web design to make money. The artwork is a chaotic collage of Multiplicity in Action Series of brightly colored abstract meanderings that explore what happens when the dominant reality is bracketed and another reality becomes possible.

Cybernetics

When I first heard of it, I thought, "Oh no, is this another type of academic area with the credibility of phrenology?" Cybernetics has more scientific integrity than phrenology. It is typically less popular with earth-oriented perspectives. Cybernetics uses systems to make work more efficient. Imagine, how can I mine a field of chaos? Ask questions, which questions? I'll make a list. From that list, I will make priorities. Can I make a system to measure if I'm mining what I want? What would be a system? What's the value of a system? How do I compose a system that will cause the desired outcome? All needs to be met locally and sustainably. How do I fix my house in high school, or how do I live off wild plants, make musical instruments, and do permaculture? All the world is a stage. People are 1001 treasures for you to discover. You can check to make sure you are getting what you want. You can make changes and see what happens. You can map out what you know and what you don't know. It's a method of investigating an area of chaos.

Cybernetics toolbox

Looking at my toolbox or a problem without a solution, I think, "I need a system." While the idea of a system may seem cold, machinic, and math-oriented, it's a good starting point when you come across something that's completely baffling. When your mind draws a complete blank, or you feel like you have no clue, you are finally getting somewhere. Use the following steps to make a system to solve a problem.

- **Define the domain** or limits; this is an unknown field of information or chaos.

- **Ask questions** to find out what you want to extract from the domain.
- **Answer the questions; when** all the questions are answered, there is no more information in the system.

Within the domain is a field of information. One can define what is necessary and what is superfluous within that domain. The function of the domain becomes something else; in this case, it becomes the set of tools, materials, and procedures for completing the project called moving the wall. When the wall is finished or when I've finished defining how I will do the project, the system has been exhausted, and no information will be left to extract within the system. So when I look around and find something that captures my interest, I say, "I need a system," with that system, I create the means to make action happen. I do this with my toolbox, which is called Cybernetics.

Auto Free Design

While attending the SDAS, I made two pamphlets. One, Auto Free Design, is a brief pamphlet outlining the idea of urban areas set up so that people can live without automobiles. Some core ideas are meeting needs within walking distance, reducing auto use, and providing sustainable transport infrastructure, including walkways, bike lanes, transit, and development that allows people to walk to meet needs.

Foundations of Alternative Action

This pamphlet explores composing relations and designing action to create alternatives to the dominant codes. With concrete guidelines for a philosophy of action, design, and multiplicity, it is a provocative set of ideas to facilitate defining change to the point of action.

Molecular Traces Video

Another project I did was a video called Molecular Traces. I asked students and teachers to perform answers to two questions: "Why are you involved with the SDAS, and what projects did you work on?" The responses range from a set of performances to spontaneous outbursts of inspired creativity. The video is a rough and tumbling compilation of shy and not-shy voices from the school. It's a sweet, light, rambling portrait of difference that never seems to end.

Experiments in Multimediaction

As part of a project for the School for Designing a Society, I set up Experiments in Multimediaction. While the program was ambitious and ambiguous, one person showed up. Some may say, "Well, that's an obvious failure." However, in this case, the consequences were beyond what many classes achieved with many more people. That one person was the perfect, uncommon individual who would get off the couch and engage in Pandora's box of amusing desires. Dan was a part of SDAS, so our standard references needed no introduction. Quickly, we began laying out what became the Bolozone. I was intrigued by the book Bolo Bolo and books published by Zone Publishers. These two books provided a theoretical base for the project. Combining these ideas resulted in the name the Bolozone. Another project influenced the Bolozone, Nottingham Coop in Madison, WI, which is Madison's most open and radical housing cooperative. They host the most different art, activism, and music events. Combining these ideas, Bolozone became a place for radical artists and activists to live in a neighborhood of artists in St. Louis, Missouri.

7

SQUATTING IN NEW YORK CITY

During the 1970s and 80s, New York City (NYC) was amid a downturn. The housing crisis was in full swing. Landlords couldn't make money on their buildings and had no incentive to maintain them. Some buildings started on fire, and some were abandoned after too many problems were not fixed. A group of people needed housing and moved in. Without water, gas, or electricity, they began to occupy and restore the buildings. They did this without permission from anyone. At any time within the first month of occupation, the police could evict them. These people are squatters. Few people would attempt what they were doing, especially if they could get housing in other ways. You had to be tough to live in a squat at that time. Squatters who use abandoned or neglected buildings and fix them up while living there are helping to make affordable housing.

Criminals Controlled the Streets.

I stepped off the Greyhound bus, assembled my bicycle, and road to 7th Street in the early 1980s. I had one contact in NYC. He lived in the squat between Ave B and C. I'd never been to the city, so I was intimidated and filled with butterflies. With a loaded pack and a bicycle, I headed to the last step to arrive at my destination. At 7th and B, the Street was blocked off with barricades. A large man was blocking the entrance to my only connection in the big city. Criminals had taken over the Street and blocked off the entrance to 7th Street. I told the guy I needed to get in, and he said the block was closed off and there was no way for me to get in. I told him I had to get in, and he refused. I was persistent and told him there was no way I would leave and that it was a public street, and he had to let me. I told him I was going to the squat to visit John, which was the only thing I would do. Eventually, he let me in. In his mind, I was a police officer.

How to Get In?

That was the first obstacle; more were to follow. Squats are not easy to get into. Everyone wants to get in, the police, fire department, building, inspectors, junkies, crackheads, homeless people, and squatters. This building had six floors, no intercom, and cell phones did not exist. Also, people didn't want to open the door unless they had to. If you open the door, the police could come in, or a drug addict or someone who would take over your room in the squat. After all, what would you do? Call the police? Squats are a magnet for junkies and criminals. Another barrier that made the squats challenging to enter was Morena, the dog of the house. Morena was a mix of pit bull and something else. She was highly territorial and could easily clamp her jaws around your neck and not let go until you dropped. While this never happened, perhaps 90% of the people who entered the building had dog teeth marks on their skin to prove it. So I arrived and knocked and knocked and shouted the name of my contact, and still no one answered. After what seemed like forever, my contact came out of the door and let me in. I chained my bicycle and secured my belongings as best I could. Oh, and yes, while you are trying to get in the door, the criminals see you as fresh meat, ready to steal your belongings.

Danger in the Streets

In the mid-1980s, in the East Village, criminals controlled the Street. Drug dealers would close off the Street and make payments to the police to keep them out. It was all about business, and even though they wouldn't let me on the block, once I was in and they were sure I wasn't a cop, they didn't give me any trouble. Even though a few cops were on the take, others may not have approved of the crime. Perhaps they worked with a dealer on the next block, and now it was payback time. Or what if it was a new cop who had no idea what was happening? Or what if the police had family or friends on the block and they were calling for help? Typically, the streets were infinitely dangerous. If you left anything on the Street and did not pay attention, it would be gone very quickly. If you were dumb enough to try to get it back or if you had a lot more force than a gang of hardened criminals, perhaps you could get it back, or more likely, they would beat you and take anything else in your possession. If you were going somewhere, you had to go there, not speak or look at anyone, and get to your destination and inside your building as fast as possible, double lock the door, and make sure they can't enter the fire escape windows.

Danger in the Squats

Fires were common in the squats. With no heating system, no smoke alarms, and people who may not care about anything but the next shot of dope or to get a fire going so you don't freeze to death, fires were a significant danger in the squat. 7th Street was no exception. One section of the building was burnt out. Somehow, the stairs and the other 2/3rds of the building survived the fire. You could still walk the stairs, but if you weren't careful and leaned in the wrong direction, you could fall from the public hall into the fire-damaged area. It's a 50' drop, and you would probably die or suffer endlessly from the injuries if you made it. People would rig whatever they could to get electricity for a heater. Sometimes, they would take it from a pole in the Street or building next door or run a wire from a fuse box without concern about whether it was safe enough to pass the code. Many had no idea of the danger. There were no smoke alarms, so if you lived on the upper floors and someone started a fire below, you may not have had enough warning to get out before dying from the fire. Another source of danger was the junkies and criminals who could get on your better side and steal whatever they could get their hands on and then deny what they had done, or they would blame it on someone else in the building. So, if you somehow overcame all those obstacles, you had to deal with the air quality. Because many areas were not finished, there may have been burnt-out materials around, and because the streets may not have been cleaned very often, there was a lot of stinky, cement-encrusted dust, another common danger to look out for. Also, Morena, the house dog, had 6-inch jaws, a huge appetite, and was more territorial than Hitler's army. She was so pretty, always looking for human flesh to chew on.

Danger from the Police, Fire department, and the New York City

Some laws protected the squatters from the authorities, but many police, firefighters, and emergency responders didn't want to set foot in these areas. Criminals could attack them, and the criminals could steal the vehicle, materials, and tools. The squatters knew what was at stake and put their best foot forward to resist. Once you learned the ropes, it was possible to adapt to the danger. If you could prove you had been there for 30 days, the liberal courts would not make it easy for anyone to evict you. Also, without a large contingent of police or firefighters, they could easily be outdone by the street dwellers, who knew that going to prison might be better than living in the hell called the East Village. Some had little to lose but knew the value of an apartment. They also knew that much of the public was on their side. At the time, the government had failed.

Still, the police were a significant danger. They would give notice that the eviction was going to happen. Squatters would organize to secure the building with barricades, assemble ways to fight the police and activate lawyers, protesters, and journalists. If the police weren't ready to take massive action, the squatters would win. This happened at the Umbrella house. I was there when they put out a call to action. Few people showed up, but luckily, I had a chance to use my skills to advance the squatters to victory against the police. We met one morning and built three barricades. The police would have to get through all of them to enter the building. It was fun work, but the big event was yet to happen. We secured the building to make low-income housing and another world possible. A place where people wouldn't have to slave all day to make money to pay for housing.

Fighting the police

So, we secured the building from the police. Squatters occupied the building and found another way to get in and out. The barricades were too much work to take down and put back up every time you wanted to get in and out. So, a skeleton crew set up to defend the building from the police. The big day was a victory for the squatters as the police lost the battle. The squatters kept improving the building and educating the public about their goals to make low-income housing and stop the city from letting housing infrastructure be destroyed.

The fire department was also a source of danger. With many fires going on, it was busy and understaffed. The fire department could extinguish a fire, only to see it happen again. The city didn't want half-burnt buildings that were unsafe or not built to code, so sometimes, the fire department would let them burn. Squatters would lose their home and belongings. Luckily, they were still alive.

Few would brave the intense world of squatting with fire, mayhem, and danger at nearly every turn. Those who did had to be tougher than nails and able to adapt, think quickly, and move fast. Can you imagine a group of squatters hosting an anarchist gathering in the middle of the mayhem? Attempts were made to unify the squatters, but many were at the forefront of a low-intensity war to secure housing and move forward to create a community of people who could own, manage, and maintain their buildings.

For people who had been to the anarchist gatherings in Chicago, Minneapolis, Toronto, and San Francisco, the next logical location of an anarchist gathering was Mexico City; imagine if 2-5 organizers from Chicago, Minneapolis, Toronto, and San Francisco would have come to Mexico City to organize for two weeks before the gathering. Efforts were made to do that, but it has yet to happen. Money was sent, and it disappeared. Yes, in Fantasy Land, you can send money and some resources, and somehow, it comes together if the organizers and community are intact enough to make it happen, but that was different in Mexico City in 1990. It takes organizers with experience and community to make these gatherings happen. Compared to New York City, Chicago, Minneapolis, Toronto, and San Francisco were privileged places compared to what the squatters in NYC were dealing with. Taking over buildings in the capital of capitalism, the belly of the beast, was a constant struggle on many fronts. In the non-NYC cities, the affluence and safety of the anarchists there allowed them the privilege to put on gatherings. Unfortunately, they couldn't happen again as they did from 1986-1989. Somehow, things disintegrated.

Contradiction

There's a contradiction of anarchists having a centralized gathering. It could lead them into the hands of the police, so they would have to have a coherent plan. They were organized in Chicago. When the police came, the settlers left and cut their losses. The community of people were able to carry on. If they had tried to defend the building against the police, many of the community may have been beaten up and put in prison, and the building destroyed. So, the center of activity is typically raided before the events happen. The two forces coexist in the bigger scheme of things, even as the planet marches on with more development.

Victory in the East Village

After years of negotiating with the city, the squatters negotiated to take ownership of the buildings. The city required the squatters to bring the buildings up to code. In between the city and the squatters was a group called the Urban Homesteading Assistance Board (UHAB). They negotiated the agreement and helped to keep the buildings maintained and functioning. UHAB helps the squatters renovate and maintain the buildings.

8

SCHIZ-FLUX

I dropped out of college for two reasons. The first is because I didn't want a job in the capitalist economy. Second, I wanted to be something other than an indentured servant to college debt. I wanted to be educated and knew I didn't have to pay a fortune. Which way to go? I had spent a year at the university, worked at the fusion reactor lab, and lived in a commune. It was a good life. I could work part-time, study, and have a decent life without slaving for the machine. I wanted a university education, so I began auditing classes. Some classes had hundreds of students and didn't take attendance. I made a list of classes, attended them, took notes and read the books. For the writing part of my do-it-yourself degree, I made a zine with friends. I put the word out and found people with interest. One day, I was sitting on a small hill on campus, and this guy dropped out of the sky before me. This was a sign of talent.

Inchoate Beginnings

We talked, shared stories, and kept moving. Someone told me I should meet this guy. It's still a mystery how we met, how I came to all of this, or how I could be at the center of things; after all, I was pretty new to university life. I had some notion of the university but had yet to learn how fake it was. Most students were there for reasons other than a fierce pursuit of something worth knowing. Many were there to fulfill a path made by their parents. They would go to school, find a job, get married, have children, and become part of the system. From an early age, I rebelled against nearly anything conventional. It was a never-ending recipe for boredom, conformity, and a dull, empty life without anything worth doing. That's just the point: what is worth doing? If you accept things as they are, there's no reason to look for anything else, to experiment and fail and keep going, trying to make something beyond here and now. I was on that path. For now, we had to get the magazine finished.

Breaking the Codes

I had no clear idea where I was coming from or going to. That's why we were doing the zine. Drake had more experience with all of this. He had his degree, had worked with Lyx and Miekal, and had more confidence in all of this. It was all too new for me to be comfortable with. The first issue of our zine was a rant-filled poetic slam against the dominant codes. None of us used our names in the writing we did. Somehow, we were against all of that. Nothing was original; nothing was created. Everything came from the social world. We are social; nothing is personal, and no one can make anything. All are social; all work is social. New ideas are impossible. All of us assumed the name Karen Elliot. We move through the codes of behavior. The dominant society was on a dead-end path. Somehow, we had to come up with a name.

Schiz-Flux

Deleuze and Guattari wrote some of my favorite books. One was A Thousand Plateaus, another Capitalism and Schizophrenia. The ideas were not linear, perhaps more literary and poetic. Challenging the codes of conformity with more logic didn't make sense. They understood logic, and if we were understood, we could be undermined. Also, Semiotext used the name Schiz in some of their books. Schizophrenia was dangerous for the dominant codes. Using the first word for half of the group's name implied a danger to the status quo. Flux was related to the Fluxus group. I was a welder, and flux is used in welding to fuse metals. Our tendencies were close to Fluxus, so when we came up with the name Schiz-Flux, it worked well enough to continue to use it. It was dangerous with a creative spin. The name fits the material and was original enough to go beyond most other action areas.

D-rake and I were the core of the group. He was more of a frontman and show-off. I was more practical, connected to the earth, and introverted. Somehow, it all fits together. The theory had to meet practice. Defining what that meant was more than a challenge. I was in my early 20s and was involved in working-class action most of my life. I had learned carpentry and welding and knew nothing about philosophy, Marxism, and going beyond the dominant codes. All of this was new. I needed more, if any, grounding in political theory. I had just found the housing coops, the most liberating entity I could find. I wanted to be in a worker's union but had no means. I was against work. Work supported the dead-end economy. Unions were conservative institutions. We were on the edge of theory and action, art and politics. The default actions I was involved with were the housing cooperatives and the avant guard at 1341.

Was And

Liz Was, and Miekal ran an avant-garde operation out of a house on Willy Street in Madison. I heard the call for action on the radio. I show up at 1341, and they put me right to work. There she was, full of life; Liz Was on the porch of 1341. She was upbeat, energetic, and open. Miekal had a later focus and quickly gave me something to do, which I could appreciate. He brought me to the backyard with an old piano. My first art project was dismantling the piano and making it naked to be used more like a harp or to bang on and create a sound. We were making instruments and swamp creatures to combat the Festival of the Lakes, a city-sponsored art fest that paid big money for famous people to perform and ignored local artists. I went with the flow of what was happening. Liz and Miekal were motivated and creative and constantly broke the codes. I needed to be aware of something else to get involved. We put our energy into the best project we could find. Schiz-Flux actions were partially defined.

War Chest Tour

As time passed, the orientation of our group became more focused. Without a driving purpose and enough discussions to define a coherent set of actions, we put together some ideas to make action happen. Drake had been doing this for a while. He was comfortable speaking to people with a bullhorn in public. I had never done that. He could talk in front of reporters. He'd been naked in public. He worked with Liz and Miekal and performed in front of people. He was comfortable in this role. I didn't have enough time to be afraid. My interpretation of the tour contained a lot more art, perhaps moving walls of art.

After working with L &f M and the festival of the Swamps, I was art-focused and came to the action obliquely. I needed more conversation and attention to define the action adequately. I was confused and beyond overwhelmed. I began assembling 2 x 2 x 6-foot stiles and rolls of uncommon plastic 4' x 20 feet of 5 mil plastic, and then the idea was to paint or collage images of a desired community. I needed more confidence in my idea, but there were too many unanswered questions, intense hesitations, and impossible deadlines. I wasn't a graphic artist and required more time or organizing skills to make it happen. So the action started in a 1/2 hour. I had no idea what would happen. Ultimately, I may have grabbed a sax and met them at the student union. We were going to smoke pot in the student union, then go on an avant-garde parade, then to targets to bring attention to the war-making institutions in the neighborhood. The ideas weren't clear; for Drake, it was child's play. He did these super complicated performances, doing things no one would ever consider pleasant and not without the highest merit for original composition beyond the edge.

SMILE magazine

A group of us came together to work on SMILE magazine. Someone had to pull it all together and ensure the work was done. The zine was a challenge.

I started without a base of knowledge and practice when we started this zine. I had to learn a lot and had little guidance. I didn't have mentors or go to school for journalism and didn't learn much of it in high school. It was a zine, the best efforts of the untrained. The zine was called SMILE. A group of us came together to make it happen.

We were minimally organized at best. We didn't try to resolve our political differences. It was inchoate and gradually formed more focus and coherence as more zines were produced. With a red cover on the first issue of the SMILE zine, it was an attention grabber. People submitted what they wanted. There was some coherence, but it was more a combination of submissions.

9

DREAMTIME

A group of us started a project called Dreamtime Village in rural Wisconsin. Toward the end of the 1980's, a transition was upon us. Growing pressure from the city, landlord, and neighborhood pushed us out. Gentrification was taking over the neighborhood. Across the Street was a fantastic art house. Human-size and larger sculptures covered in mosaic tile, broken glass, and mirror fragments occupied the two-story house for decades. The artist, Mona, traveled the world and materialized her experiences in the house. After she died, no one was willing to take over. After the home sold, the project ended. The wobblies, with a printing press across the Street, were pushed out. Somehow, Lyx and McKel beat back the police, code enforcement, and landlord for years, turning the building inside and outside into an avant-garde museum of art.

1341

In Madison, we had this building at 1341 Williamson. The locals called it Willy Street. It was a beat-up old house on a busy street. There were three bedrooms and one or two bathrooms. Lyx and McKel trans-formed the building into an avant-garde art factory. The upstairs bedroom was used to make books, and the downstairs living room was transformed into a music room. Two or three rooms were used for bedrooms. Inside and outside of the building, the walls were covered with art. We made a two-story sculpture called the church of Anarchy in the front yard. Someone, probably Lyx and McKel, made a 3' x 6' portrait of a person and filled it in with used mail art stamps. It was an art playhouse. Lyx and Mckel grew giant gourds in the backyard to make musical instruments and large outdoor sculptures.

I had my bus against the back of the property. A large tow truck snuck it in the back. Oh, and yes, there was a little space for car parking. Scorned by the Better Homes and Gardens type people and loved by the poets, artists, and intellectuals, the house was a magnet for the counter culture that never died after the 60s. Toward the end of the 1980's, the forces of gentrification gathered momentum. With the land-lord beating down, Lyx and McKel planned for another life in the countryside. There was not enough to make a life worth living in Madison. I began hearing about living in the country and setting up another project.

Transition

Getting stoned and talking about Utopia was typically the closest we could get to making wet dreams real. Taking acid every day didn't work. Gradually, reality began to hit the fan. I went to the East Coast to experience Bread and Puppet theatre. On the way, I met this woman on the Greyhound bus. She told me about this guy looking for people to move to the country. It was unclear what it was about, so I got the number for the guy, and Lyx and McKel moved into high gear to pursue another future. By the time I had hitchhiked back from the East Coast, they had a meeting with this guy, Keith. He was an anomaly, and we didn't know what was happening. He flashed money, took us to dinner, and floated lofty ideas of transforming the rural area into a stoner's Utopia. At that time, Keith had befriended an elderly lady who was funding the project. It was in a small dying town called West Lima, Wisconsin. There were three houses in town and two properties within 10 miles. And did I mention there was a school? Eventually, Lyx and Miekal negotiated for us to move out there and begin the rural transformation.

Setting Up

Gradually, around 1990, we went to West Lima and brought art supplies, instruments, tools, and belongings to the two houses. One is called the post office, and the other is the hotel. The buildings became homes after the town lost most of its population. Finally, the day came when 1341 was over. The landlord took the house back, and another icon of resistance fell. First were the wobblies, then Mona's house, and now 1341, the last base to bash the dominant codes, undermine ossified patterns, and counter the better homes and gardens effluvia. Let the weeds grow, leaves nourish the soil, and the bees and the nightcrawlers take action! We went to the country.

Permaculture

From the grapevine, I found out about Permaculture or permanent agriculture. It's an inspiration for many people. The book illustrates how to maximize beneficial relations between the ecosystem, plants, animals, and people. It seeks to help people grow food from the ground to the top of the trees. It's a method of experimenting with ecosystems to maximize the benefits. We are permanently changing and permanently adapting. So I brought the book to Lyx & Mckel, and he ran with it. Permaculture is an idea that maximizes the growing potential in an area and teaches people to use what is local and what proliferates. There are many ways to interpret Permaculture. We planted many trees and perennials and hosted permaculture design courses at Dreamtime Village.

Permaculture Design Course

Shortly after we arrived, we set up, organized, and finished a permaculture design course. Somehow, the three of us pulled it off. Lyx and McKel set up the instructors and students. I helped to organize and facilitate housing and food. We participated in the event. It was a thoughtful and strategic move. It enabled us to harvest the design ideas of the instructors and participants. We began to realize how difficult it is to implement extravagant designs. The course allowed us to come up with many ideas. It lasted two weeks and had about 15 participants. Classes focused on ways to grow plants and animals to harmonize beneficial relationships. In groups of 3-5 people, we worked on a design for ten days, and on the last day, the groups presented their designs.

Nomadic Circuit

Got culture? Culture happens with difference. Dreamtime attracted nomads from around the states. With ample space to camp or use a room in the hotel, we could host 5-20 people. Located between Chicago and Minneapolis in the middle of the country, it was a good stopping point for people going from coast to coast. Musicians, artists, writers, and activists brought music, art, and culture. They would stop for a few days to a couple of weeks. We embraced alternative culture, which included fire-breathing, circus performances, avant-garde music, composition, punk rock, and almost anything that did not prop up the dominant system. This made Dreamtime exciting.

Making Music Instruments

The culture of music and art is robust at Dreamtime Village. Lyx and McKell were musicians who weren't afraid of pushing the limits. They also like to make things. They grew gourds and made string and percussion instruments with them. Morgan set up a business to make drums for five or seven years. We made Djembes and Ashiko drums, and Djam from Ghana did the carving. For inspiration and instructions, we read "Experimental Musical Instruments". People come to Dreamtime Village to make musical instruments. Some people use whatever materials are available to make an instrument.

Rural challenges

Dreamtime Village is a nonprofit project. It depends on volunteer labor. Since it is in the countryside with few people, there's a lot of work to do but little money for labor. If this project was in New York City, many volunteers with excellent skills would be there. To buy anything usually requires owning, operating, and maintaining a vehicle. This is quite expensive for people living in a rural area. It's possible to bicycle, but there are many hills and some steep. This would be even more difficult in the winter when the snow and ice arrive. Also, most people want to avoid taking such a risk. Bicycles are uncommon; some people car drivers might flip out when they see one.

People who wish to visit must either get a car or have someone drive them. There needs to be more public transportation there.

Uncommon Intimacy

Rural locations can offer some things you don't get in a big city. It's one experience to meet someone in New York City and a very different experience to meet them at Dreamtime Village. People are very busy in the city and have their guard up. Their minds are racing to the next moment. At Dreamtime, there's more time for people to engage face-to-face. With fewer distractions, events, and offerings, people have more time to relax and hang out with each other.

Transportation

Living in a rural area has many advantages: lower-cost housing, wood for heating, and ample space to grow food. The air is better, there are abundant wild plants, and there is more room to grow and raise animals. All this depends on transportation—a new vehicle costs around $1000 per month. People own used vehicles. They are unlikely to own and operate the car for under $200 a month.

Infrastructure

The central infrastructures of Dreamtime Village are buildings. These buildings need to be maintained. The older the buildings get, the more maintenance they need; sometimes, the systems must be replaced. The roof goes bad and is rotting, and if that's not fixed, the building will collapse quickly, especially if there's a lot of snow and rain mixed. More people and money are needed to maintain the buildings at Dreamtime Village. The members need help economically. Some are well-worn and getting closer to the edge, but luckily, more people are willing to participate. We need people, but only a few know about the opportunity. People need good jobs. Some remote workers may like living there. If we got a huge grant, we could pay people to fix up the buildings while they live there. We would have to have jobs for them and housing. They could fix up one building and keep going until all of them are finished. I've got to raise $2 million. I will stop wasting my time getting moving.

Into the future

Dreamtime Village is an experiment that transforms everyday life. Another future rises in the hustle and bustle in the belly of the beast. A group of us left the city to establish an area in the countryside for Permaculture, art, and design to flourish. We set up the conditions for artists, activists, writers, and designers of the future to explore, connect with nature, and make a life worth living. Who wants to toil endlessly and have no housing, security, healthcare, and a dead-end life of endless production to follow the machine? While many rural projects have sunk in 10 years, Dreamtime has been going on for 30 years. It's not the heyday of the first ten years, but the infrastructure is still there, and the core people keep going. Take advantage of it if you can, and check it out. You may find a spot to stay and make a life beyond the pale of the dominant codes.

ABOUT THE AUTHOR

Dan Paul grew up in Lake Wobegon fishing, playing sports and building houses. After attending the University of Wisconsin, Madison and working at the linear fusion reactor lab, he explored alternatives to the dominant codes. While staying in coops, communes, and squats around the country, he learned the fundamentals of setting up and operating progressive, radical and sustainable alternatives to the code of the corporation and nation.

f X ⊙

ALSO BY DAN PAUL

Philosophy of Action Design and Multiplicity by Dan Paul

Book 1 Auto FreeDesign

Book 2 Workers Health Handbook

Book 3 Save Your Life Prevent Hospital Use

Book 4 Coop OwnersHandbook

Book 5 Eye on AI Meeting NeedsSustainably

Book 6 Travels on the NomadicTerrain

Book 7 Tales of the UrbanShaman

Book 8 Housing in the Danger Zone

Book 9 CoronaTime

Book 10 Philosophy of Design, Action and Multiplicity

Coming soon

Landlords Against Eviction

Auto Free USA

Websites

https://viaradmedia.org

https://autofreedesign.com

http://workershealthhandbook.com

http://sylphu.com

www.ingramcontent.com/pod-product-compliance
Lightning Source LLC
Chambersburg PA
CBHW060621070426
42447CB00040B/2210